God's World
Activities for Toddlers

Illustrated by
Kathryn Marlin

Cover Illustrated by
Kathryn Marlin

All rights reserved—Printed in the U.S.A.
Copyright © 1998 Shining Star Publications
A Division of Frank Schaffer Publications, Inc.
23740 Hawthorne Blvd., Torrance, CA 90505

ISBN No. 0-7647-0484-2

Table of Contents

To Teachers and Parents

Busy, always on the go, never sitting when they can stand, never standing when they can run! Isn't that a pretty good description of most toddlers (and toddlers' mothers)? However, there are those "teachable moments" when toddlers will sit enthralled by the story you're reading or listen wide-eyed to the story you're telling. They love finding out about things and getting involved.

The activities in this book have been designed to help teachers and parents make the most of those "teachable moments." Included are important lessons and concepts that will introduce toddlers to God and His wonderful world. Poems, action rhymes, songs, learning center ideas, visuals, and simple crafts are just a few of the activities this book features. Also included are patterns, directions, materials, and any other items needed to aid in the simplicity and clarity of the activities. Each activity is brief, taking only a few minutes, so those little minds won't have time to get distracted.

Be sure to practice the rhymes and stories before trying them out with your toddlers. You shouldn't have to look at the book (that's the time when your toddlers will become distracted). It might be easier to print the words on the board or on a large piece of paper which you can mount on a wall. That way, your hands will be free to do the actions, and other adults in the room can say the words with you.

Enjoy these stimulating activities with the children as they discover God's wonderful world.

Who's in the Garden?

Read the children the story below. Then give each child a copy of the picture at the bottom of the page. Have children color each baby and its mother the same color.

God made a big beautiful garden. Do you know what was in God's garden? There were green plants, beautiful flowers, and all kinds of fruit trees.

Do you know what God decided to put in His garden next? He put animals in His garden. There were big animals, little animals, animals with fur, and animals with feathers. And the animals were all nice. They didn't bite or scratch.

God knew His garden needed one more thing. It needed people. So God made a man named Adam and a woman named Eve to take care of His garden. Adam and Eve lived in the garden. They played with the animals. Maybe they petted all the lions or had races with the tigers. Maybe they rode on some of the animals. Which animals would you ride?

Adam and Eve were happy in the garden. The animals were happy in the garden. God's big beautiful garden was a happy place to live in.

by Katrina Cassel

God Created All the Animals

Tell the children that God created all the animals—fish, birds, wild animals, farm animals, and even insects. Then He created people. He put people in charge of the animals. The first person He created was a man He named Adam. God brought the animals He had made to Adam, and Adam named them.

Say to the children, "Let's pretend to be animals, guessing what animals we are pretending to be."

Each toddler who wants to can take a turn acting like a certain animal. (You may have to suggest to the children which animal to be.) The child acts out how the animal moves and what sound it makes and the class guesses its name. Then let the whole class imitate that animal.

Optional Idea: Tell all the children to walk on their hands and knees and say "meow." Then ask the children what Adam named the animal they are imitating. Coach the children to be dogs, birds, rabbits, frogs, fish, seals, penguins, horses, elephants, bears, cows, snakes, sheep, pigs, chickens, etc.

by Marcia Noel Hornok

Wiggly Animal Pictures

Bring life to pictures about Creation. To do this, carefully cut one or two round holes in some of your animal pictures or posters. For example, cut a hole in the mouth of a snake. Poke one finger through and wiggle it to be the snake's tongue.

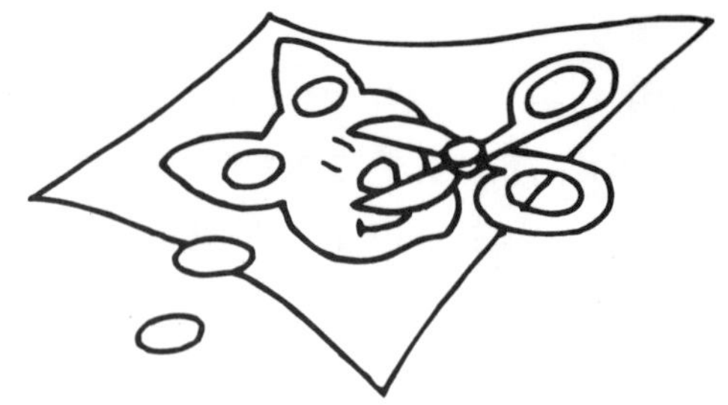

Or, cut two holes in the bottom of a rabbit's ears. Poke two fingers through and wiggle them to be the rabbit's ears. You could also cut a hole in the top of an elephant's trunk. Poke a finger through and wiggle it. The possibilities are endless!

by Mary J. Davis

SS4843

Feather and Fur Fun

What a fun way for children to learn about animals and their coverings!

Gather samples of feathers and fur for the children to see and touch. Then say to the children, "Each day when you get out of bed, you put on your clothes. Your clothes are important. They keep your body cool and protected in the summer sun and warm in the winter cold. Did you know that God dressed all animals when He created them?"

"Some animals are dressed in feathers. Feathers are soft to touch. They have tiny shafts inside them that let air circulate. Birds are dressed in feathers, and their feathers help them fly. Baby birds cannot fly until they have grown their first set of feathers. In the spring and fall, birds molt. That means their feathers fall out, and new ones grow in. God dresses them in warmer feathers for the winter, and stronger feathers to help them fly long distances when they must make their migratory flights. Hidden beneath their flying feathers are very soft feathers. These are called downy feathers. Mothers wrap these feathers around their new babies to cuddle them and keep them warm. God also created some very colorful feathers to dress up birds like peacocks and turkeys. He put a special coating on other feathers so that ducks and geese can go swimming."

"Birds live above the ground and fly through the air. That is why God dressed them in feathers. There are other animals that live on or under the ground. God dressed these animal creatures in fur. Can you think of any animals that have soft fur?"

"Some animals are named because of the color of their fur—like the black bear and the red fox. Fur keeps animals warm in the winter and cool in the summer. Furry animals don't molt like birds, but they go through shedding seasons. This means their old fur falls out and they grow new fur. Summer fur is soft and light, but winter fur is thick like a big winter coat. God created so many wonderful creatures for us to love and enjoy."

"Let's pray together: Thank You, God, for dressing animals in fancy feathers and fur. They are beautiful."

by Susan Jordan

Flashing Fireflies

Show the children a live firefly in a jar or a picture of one.

Tell the children, "Fireflies are one of God's very special little creatures. They aren't really flies. They are beetles. Fireflies have three body parts: a head, a chest, and a stomach. They have six legs, two wiggly feelers on their heads, wings, and something that makes them extra special: a flashing light! Sometimes we call them lightning bugs."

"God created fireflies with a flashing light for a reason. A firefly uses its light to attract a mate. The boy fireflies have wings and blink their lights while they are flying. The female fireflies don't have wings. They signal from the ground. A male will flash a light signal, and the female will answer back. Soon they get together, and one day, they will have a firefly family."

by Susan Jordan

Seashell Treasures

Hide several small shells in a sand pit. Children may wear protective eye covering for this activity.

Tell the children: "Each morning and evening, the ocean tides come in and goes out. When the tide comes in, small shelled sea creatures float in on the waves. When the tide goes out, the tiny shelled creatures often get stuck in the sand. They cannot get back out to the sea. People walking along the beaches will find many different kinds of shells lying on the sand. If we dig, we might be able to find some shells hiding in our sand pit."

Children may use sand-sifting toys or tea strainers to play in the sand as they discover hidden treasures.

Continue: "Each shell that you find was once the home of a tiny sea creature. How are these homes different from your home? Can you think of other animals that live in shells? (snails, turtles) What colors and shapes are the shells? Are they big or small? Are they soft, smooth, round, or pointed?"

"Let's all pray. Thank You, God, for creating sea creatures and their beautiful homes!"

by Susan Jordan

Homespun Toys

This activity will help the children see all the natural "toys" God has made.

Gather a collection of nature items native to your area. (Examples: a walnut shell, an acorn top, a dandelion, a maple helicopter, a long blade of grass, a milkweed pod, flat stones, a feather, honeysuckle flowers, a container of mud) Demonstrate how to play with the items as you talk about them. Display the items on a table. Say to the children, "Can you see all the wonderful toys just waiting to be played with? God created all these wonderful toys for us to enjoy."

Tell the children that many years ago, there were no toy stores, so children played with things they found outdoors. A walnut shell and a milkweed pod can be tiny boats that sail in a creek. An acorn top can fit on your finger and make a moving doll, a wiggly talking puppet, or a whistle.

Dandelions and maple helicopters are almost as fun to blow and catch as a jar of bubbles! Long blades of grass pressed between two fingers make loud whistles. Flat stones can skip and bounce if you throw them over water just right. Ask the children if they have ever baked mud cakes and let them dry in the sun. They are fun to make, but not to taste! Ask the children if they would like to have a tea party and serve tasty honeysuckle treats. They're delicious to lick! God made the best toys and surprises just outside the door. See if the children can find some other toys hiding in their backyards!

by Susan Jordan

What Living Things Do

Children love to answer questions and make noises. Lead the children in this question/answer activity by doing both parts or by asking the questions and having another adult lead the children in the responses.

Question	**Response**
What do stars do?	Twinkle, twinkle. (Open and close hands above head.)
What do fish do?	Swish, swish.
What do birds do?	Fly, fly. (Flap arms.)
What do frogs do?	Hop, hop.
What do snakes do?	Hiss, hiss.
What do bees do?	Buzz, buzz.
What do worms do?	Wiggle, wiggle.
What do trees do?	Stretch, stretch.
What do teachers do?	Smile, smile.
What do children do?	Praise the Lord. (Clap and dance.)

by Marcia Noel Hornok

Corn-fusing Treats

Gather a variety of items that are corn products: popcorn, corn dogs, corn chips, corn on the cob, Indian corn, creamed corn, corn flakes, corn kernels, corn tortillas. Tell the children to look at all of these things. They all look different. They all taste different. But all of these things come from corn. Explain to the children what happens: When a farmer plants one corn kernel in the ground, a cornstalk grows. Soon ears of corn grow on the cornstalk. By the end of summer, the ears of corn are ready for picking.

After the corn is harvested, it can be fixed many ways. It can be ground into cornmeal and used to make corn dogs, tortillas, chips, and flakes. Sometimes corn is cooked on the cob. Ask the children if they like corn on the cob. Explain that the kernels can be cut off the cob and used for sweet corn, creamed corn, or even popcorn.

God knows that we all like to eat different kinds of things, and that's one reason He created corn. He knew it could be fixed in many ways for a lot of different tastes. Ask the children how they like to eat corn.

Pray together: "Thank You, God, for creating corn!"

by Susan Jordan

note: This lesson on corn could also be compared to the diet of manna the nation of Israel ate for 40 years! It was the same food fixed in a great variety of ways for the enjoyment of all.

Shout for Joy

The children can learn all about the wonderful sounds in nature in this activity. Take the children outside before you begin.

Tell the children, "God was happy after He made us all. In the Bible, He says to shout for joy. Let's all shout. (Shout names, 'I'm happy,' 'Yoo-hoo'—anything to get happy sounds.) Not all of the things God made can shout, but they can make sounds when they're happy or sounds that make us happy. What does your dog do when it's happy? What sound does your kitten make when it's happy? Now let's be quiet for a minute and listen for other sounds of things God made."

Children may hear birds singing, wind in leaves, locusts buzzing, a brook trickling, other children laughing, etc.

by Edith Cutting

13

The Four Seasons

Make copies of the pictures of the seasons below for the children. Talk about how the pictures are different. Discuss the kind of weather we usually see in each season. Talk about the colors we see in each season. Then let the children color the pictures. (For more season fun, see page 44 and let the children sing the song, "Four Seasons of a Garden.")

SS4843

Creation Classroom

Use the ideas below and on page 16 for centers or as a different activity each day or week. Plan a whole month or quarter around the Creation theme. If you have the space, leave all the centers and wall decorations up throughout the entire Creation unit.

Creation Pictures

Gather Bible teaching pictures about Creation and the first family. Make an attractive bulletin board or decorate an entire wall with the pictures. Add magazine cutouts of nature scenes, families, and animals. Refer to this grouping of pictures often. Allow children to touch the pictures. (Place the pictures low enough so that young children can touch them.) Add pictures that the children "scribble color."

Discovery Centers

Have centers or tables that feature the following activities:

- Water Fun

  A tub of water and some boats will provide hours of fun for children. Fill a spray bottle with water. Let the children spray newsprint that is spread out on a table. Encourage children to pretend to water flowers, make rain, etc.

- Dirt Fun

  Help children fill containers with dirt and pretend to plant seeds. You may also have them plant real seeds and let them grow.

- Sand

  Provide containers for children to fill and empty with sand. Small cars, trucks, and construction toys will give children opportunities for creative play. Wet some sand and give the children candy or cookie molds to fill and turn out onto paper.

  Let children make texture pictures by painting glue on paper and sprinkling on sand.

Creation Classroom (continued)

Animal World

- Provide pictures of several different animals. Place stuffed animals around the room or in the center area. As the children play, talk to them about the names of the animals. Remind children that God made every animal. Point out each one's unique features.

- Place pictures of adult and baby animals on a table. Let the children match each mommy to her baby.

- Provide pictures of animals for children to color or paint using cotton swabs and water tinted slightly with food coloring.

My Body Center

- Provide pictures of children at play, eating a meal, at church, and other activities common to children. Discuss the various activities and how we use our bodies in each one. (Examples: eating, reading, listening, coloring, baking a cake, riding a tricycle)

- Do some fun activities such as simple exercises, action rhymes, etc., in which children use their bodies in a variety of ways.

by Mary J. Davis

Pet Parade

Send a note home to parents and ask them to send their child's favorite stuffed animal to class. Cut a piece of cardboard for each child and tie a long loop of yarn to the front of it. Children can place their "pets" on the cardboard and pull them with the yarn as if pulling wagons. Have them march in a circle to favorite music with their "pet wagons."

by Mary J. Davis

Be Gentle With Your Pets

After the parade is over, seat children in a circle with their stuffed animals. Ask them what real pets they have at home. Discuss how to treat pets (pet them gently, feed and water them, love them, etc.). Then sing the words below together to the tune of "She'll Be Comin' 'Round the Mountain."

Oh, be gentle with your pets, little ones. (clap, clap)

Oh, be gentle with your pets, little ones. (clap, clap)

For the Father up above (point to heaven)

Has created them with love. (cross chest with arms)

So be gentle with your pets, little ones. (clap, clap)

by Teresa Von Busch

God Made Our Pets

A Group Participation Bulletin Board

Directions:

1. Decorate the bulletin board background as shown below.
2. Enlarge the pet patterns on page 19 to fit on your bulletin board.
3. Color the pets and cut them out.

Group Activity:

1. Hold up the pets one at a time.
2. Have the children identify each pet.
3. Ask, "Who made dogs?" Children should answer, "God made dogs."
4. Talk about where the dog should be placed on the board.
5. Attach the dog to the board in the appropriate place. Then talk about the next pet.
6. Let the children talk about their pets.

by Gayle Vella

Pet Patterns

Terrific Trees

Hey, diddle, diddle,

The big   (Raise both arms over head in a circle.)

And the little;   (Place fingertips together, forming a small circle.)

The short,   (Stoop down.)

And the fat,   (Hold arms out at sides, indicating wideness.)

And the high.   (Standing on toes, reach up with both arms.)

God made the trees that
shake in the breeze   (Shake your body.)

And raise leafy arms
to the sky.   (Raise arms overhead and wave them gently.)

by Marcia Noel Hornok

God Made Pines and Spruces

The children will love trying to be tall like trees and flying like birds!

God made pines and spruces,	(Point hands over head.)
And hemlocks evergreen.	(Point hands over head.)
He made them full of branches	(Open hands wide like spreading branches.)
In which the birds are seen.	(Move arms up and down.)

by Lois Putnam

note: Bring pictures of pines, spruces, and other evergreens to show the children. Ask them if they have any of these kinds of trees in their yards or neighborhoods. Ask them what happens to the leaves of most trees in the autumn. (They fall off.) Explain that these trees are called evergreens because they never lose all their leaves (needles) and show bare branches like other trees. That's one reason birds like them. They can stay in them year-round and be protected and safe.

We're Trees!

What a fun way to let the children pretend to be trees!

We're trees, we're trees,
Swaying in the breeze.

(Lift arms and sway back and forth.)

Now it's autumn and we're

(Shake arms.)

Dropping our leaves.

It's winter. No more leaves.

(Hold out hands, palms up, and shake head.)

We're very cold. And then

(Shiver and wrap arms around body.)

Suddenly, it's spring!

(Stretch arms up, open hands, and smile.)

We have leaves again!

by Bonnie Compton Hanson

note: After acting out the poem with the children, have them fold their hands, close their eyes, and pray, "Thank You, God, for trees."

Thunderstorms

Use the action rhymes below to help the children enjoy a
thunderstorm.

God made the lightning

Bright as a flash.   (Cover eyes.)

Then He made thunder,   (Reach hands high.)

Crash, crash, crash!   (Clap hands.)

Then He made the rain come down,

Splash, splash, splash!   (Stomp feet.)

For this action rhyme, bring a simple bouquet of dandelions or daisies.

God makes thunder,

Boom, boom, boom!   (For "Booms," pound fists together.)

Then He sends the rain   (For rain, lift arms and lower them
                                      with fingers wiggling.)

To make flowers bloom.   (Give each child a flower.)

by Edith Cutting

Raindrops and Flowers

Let's be the raindrops falling down,

Down, down, down, right to the ground.

Now let's be flowers, one by one,

Growing, growing up to the sun!

(Stand up. Reach arms up, then slowly move . . .

them down until you're crouching low.)

(Move slowly back up, until you're . . .

stretching as high as possible.)

by Bonnie Compton Hanson

Note: Read through the poem once. Then talk about rain with the children. Ask: "Do you like rain? What happens if you stand in the rain? Aren't you glad God made rain to help everything grow?"

God Made It All

The earth is round. | (Make a large circle.)

The sea is deep. | (Hold hands spaced out, one above the other, palms facing.)

The ocean is wide. | (Spread arms wide.)

The mountain is steep. | (Make hands meet overhead, forming a mountain peak.)

God made everything from shore to shore. | (Make hands do ocean waves.)

I wonder what heaven holds in store! | (Take finger and touch temple in wonder.)

by Susan Jordan

    SS4843

God Is Great!

God is great.

(Say with feeling; sweep hands in front of self.)

He is King,
Maker of
Everything!

So to Him
Let us now
Bend our knees;
Let us bow . . .

(Point up; get on knees.)

To worship Him
And to say,
"How we love You,
Lord, today!"

(Raise folded hands higher and higher.)

by Lois Putnam

From Psalm 95:3, 6

For the Lord is the great God, the great King above all gods . . . Come, let us bow down in worship, let us kneel before the LORD our Maker.

Thank You, Lord!

Thank You, Lord,
That before I came,
You knew me;
You knew my name.
And thank You, Lord,
That You made me
Very special—
Wonderfully!

(Fold hands in prayer.)

(Point to self.)

(Wrap arms around self and
move side to side.)

by Lois Putnam

SS4843

Animal Lace-ups

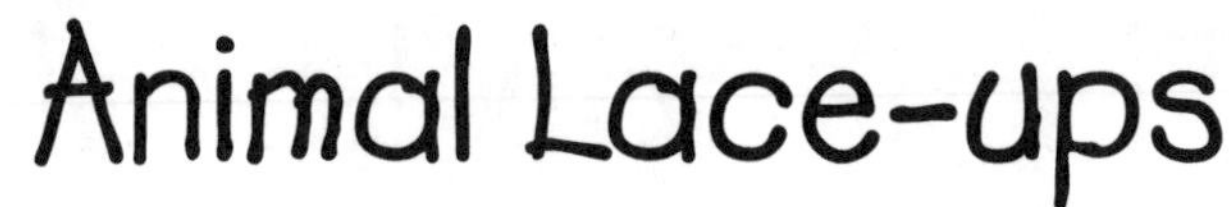

Create these simple lacing cards to be used over and over.

Materials:

pictures of animals
large colored index cards
glue
yarn
tape
hole punch

Directions:

1. Glue one animal picture on each index card.

2. Punch holes around the edge of each card.

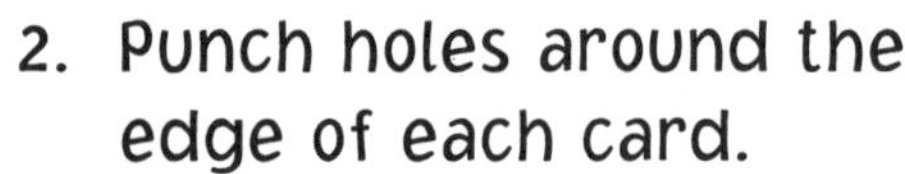

3. Cut a length of yarn that will lace easily through each hole in the card.

4. Put one end of the yarn through one of the holes and tie a knot.

5. Put a small piece of tape around the other end for easy lacing.

As children work with the lace-ups, discuss how each animal was made by God.

by Mary J. Davis

Animal Stackers

The children can learn all about the wonderful animals God created in this activity.

Materials:

a variety of empty boxes (cake mix, gelatin, and cracker boxes)

pictures of different animals

plain wrapping paper in bright colors (or brown butcher paper)

tape

glue

scissors

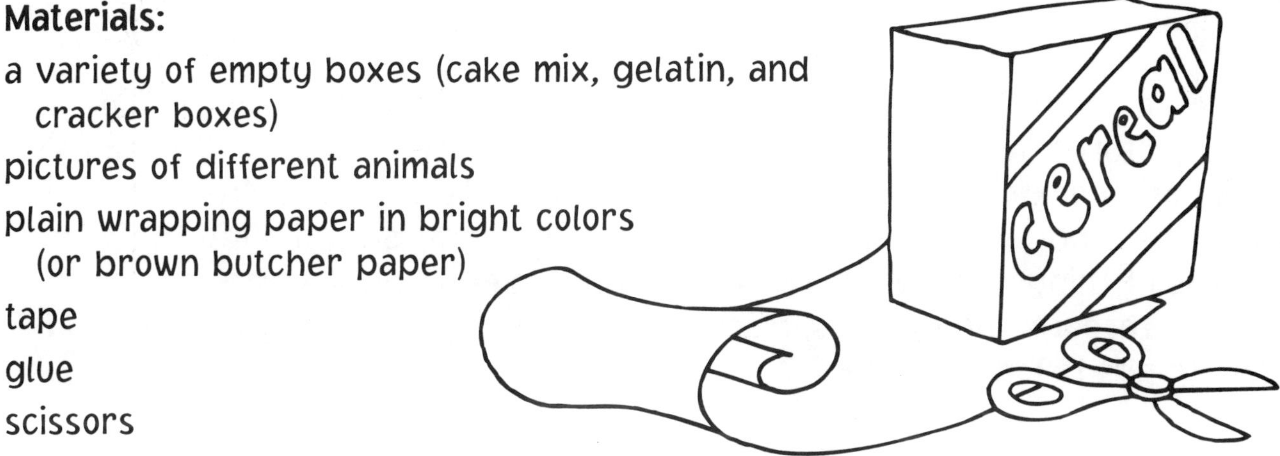

Directions:

1. Tape all boxes closed and wrap them with the plain wrapping paper.
2. Glue an animal picture on the front of each box.
3. Let the children stack the boxes, then knock them down.
4. As the children handle each box, encourage them to say the name of the animal. Remind them that God created everything.

by Mary J. Davis

Earth and Sea Books

Collect an assortment of pictures that display land and water things: animals, vehicles, plants, vegetation, people. You will need two scrapbooks. Title one scrapbook "Earth Things" and the other "Sea Things."

Spread all the pictures out for the children to see. Have the children look at all the pictures. Ask them to help you separate them. Explain to the children that in one book, we will put pictures of things that belong on the land. Fasten the land pictures into the "Earth Things" scrapbook. Fasten the pictures of things that belong in water in the "Sea Things" scrapbook. As you sort through the pictures, discuss why some things belong on land and other things belong in water.

Tell the children: "God created a wonderful world. Everything He created has a special place. When God created the earth and seas, the plants and animals, and people, He knew that each would need a special place to live. Trees need to live on the ground, but seaweed needs to live in water. People need to breathe air and live on land. Sea horses need oceans full of water so they can gallop along. God is a wonderful God. Everything He created was very good! Don't you agree?"

by Susan Jordan

Note: Scrapbooks can be made using construction paper and posterboard covers tied together with yarn.

SS4843

Nature Crowns

For this activity, each child will need a newspaper hat or a plain paper hat.

Take the children outside to collect an assortment of nature items. They may pick grass, flowers, leaves, small pine cones, small twigs, bird feathers, etc. Help them glue the items on their paper hats.

Say to the children, "God created many beautiful things for us to enjoy. He is pleased when we stop and look at the beautiful things in our world. Today, you have made nature crowns. One day, God will give you a new crown. It is called the Crown of Life. What do you think the Crown of Life will look like?"

by Susan Jordan

Feltboard Pairs

Gather pairs of objects of living things (examples—pairs of animals, flowers, two trees, a man and woman, etc.). Glue felt or sandpaper to the back of each figure. Arrange the figures in random order on a feltboard.

Say to the children, "When God created the earth and all living things on the earth, He knew it was good for each one to have a friend. God created us with needs. People need one another. Animals need one another. All living things need other living things. There are male and female animals, fish, and people. Can you find the matching pairs and put them next to each other?"

by Susan Jordan

"God Made the Weather" Paper Dolls

The children will learn all about God's weather and what to wear in it in this fun activity!

Enlarge the patterns below to make a boy or girl paper doll for each child. If possible, copy the dolls on lightweight cardboard or posterboard and cover them with clear adhesive plastic. Also copy the clothes for each child and cover them with clear adhesive plastic.

As you talk about the different kinds of weather God gives us, the children may put the appropriate clothing on their dolls.

by Mary J. Davis

SS4843

Nature Wreaths

Collect a variety of seeds, nuts, pine cones, leaves, mosses, and flowers. A class wreath can be crafted on a disposable meat tray, wooden form, Styrofoam™ ring, or a woven grapevine base. Let the children choose which items to put on the wreath. Use the wreath as a reminder of the many wonderful things God created.

by Susan Jordan

Note: You could also cut a green construction paper wreath for each child and let the children glue some of the nature items on their wreaths.

Creation "Big Book"

Oversized books are great to use with a group of children. Let the children create their own big books about Creation.

Materials:

pieces of posterboard cut in half

Creation teaching posters from Sunday school curriculum (or any large pictures of animals, people, and nature)

glue

hole punch

three or four metal rings

Directions:

1. Glue one big picture to each piece of posterboard.

2. Punch three or four holes in the left side of each piece.

3. Form a book by using the rings to hold the posterboard pages together.

by Mary J. Davis

Note: Use the animal pictures as you sing these words to the tune of "Old MacDonald Had a Farm": "God created animals many years ago. He created <u>name of animal</u> many years ago. With an 'Arf, arf,' here, and an 'Arf, arf' there. Here an 'Arf,' there an 'Arf,' everywhere an 'Arf, arf.' God created animals many years ago."

God's World
Cookie Cutter Mural

What a perfect way to let children know that they are special!

Materials:

newsprint or brown butcher paper

*tempera paints spread thin on paper plates

cookie cutters (gingerbread people, stars, moons, flowers, animals)

Directions:

1. Help the children dip their cookie cutters into the paint and press them onto the mural.

2. The children may also add handprints and footprints.

3. Stress that God made everything, and God made each of us very special.

*Alternative for paints: strawberry or chocolate flavored syrup

by Mary J. Davis

Wonderful World

Use this poem to let the children share the joy of all the wonderful things God made. Have them draw pictures of their favorite things He made.

I love the day; I love the night.
I love all the colors dark and bright.
So many pretty things to see—
God made them all for you and me!

I love the birds; I love the bees.
I love the flowers; I love the trees.
I love the sun; I love the shade.
Oh, thank You, God, for all You've made!

I love the clouds; I love the sky.
I love valleys and mountains high.
I love fall, winter, summer, spring.
Oh, thank You, God, for everything!

by Mary Christie Craig

  SS4843

Colors

Children love all the colors in God's world and this poem reinforces them.

God made lots of colors	(Hold up a few different colors of paper, cloth, crayons, etc.)
And gave us eyes to see.	(Hold up one primary color.)
What color is this? What color is this?	(Continue asking and showing the color three or four times.)
What color do you like to see?	(Give each child a piece of blank paper and a crayon of the color chosen to make whatever picture he or she likes.)

by Edith Cutting

God's Rain

This is a funny poem to read to the children. Have them draw pictures of things the rain helps make grow.

It's funny how the rain starts
With a drop or two, then three,
And soon it's raining lots of drops
On my friends and me.

We run inside and look at how
The rain comes racing down.
Soon it's raining everywhere
With puddles all around.

It isn't long until the rain
Stops coming down so fast;
And look! There are just a few small drops,
For now the shower's passed.

How beautiful the sun is when
God sends the clouds away.
Just in time for all of us
To go back out and play!

by Mary Christie Craig

SS4843

"Twinkle" Rhyme

". . . let your light shine before men, that they may see your good deeds and praise your Father in heaven." Matthew 5:16

Just as the stars do God's bidding, we, too, can do what God wants us to. Teach children the poem below or sing it to the tune of "Twinkle, Twinkle, Little Star."

Twinkle, twinkle, little star,
In the sky so very far.
   I can see the light from you
   Shining like God wants you to.
Twinkle, twinkle, little star,
In the sky so very far.

Twinkle, twinkle, like a star,
Others see us as we are.
   I can be a candle, too,
   Shining like God wants me to.
Twinkle, twinkle, like a star,
Others see us as we are.

by Marcia Noel Hornok

God Made Everything

Sing the words below to the tune of "The ABC Song" and teach the children all about what God made.

God made fingers.	(Wiggle fingers.)
God made toes.	(Wiggle toes.)
God made girls.	(Point to girls.)
And God made boys.	(Point to boys.)
God made rocks	(Make a fist like a hard rock.)
And big shade trees,	(Stand like a giant tree.)
Croaking frogs,	(Squat like a frog in a pond.)
And itchy fleas.	(Scratch body.)
God made everything	(Motion to everything around you.)
You see.	
That includes	
You and me!	(Point to self and others.)
YEAH!	(Shout!)

by Susan Jordan

The Color Song

Sing the words below to the tune of "A Hunting We Will Go." Sing the song several times, encouraging children to look around the room for orange items. After you have sung the song, let the children name the orange items. Then change to another color, and then another.

I'm looking for some orange.

I'm looking for some orange.

Where can I find something

That's colored brightly orange?

by Susan Jordan

SS4843

God Created Duckies!

Sing the words below to the tune of "Who Did Swallow Jonah?" or
say it as a lively rhyme. Put a different animal in the song each
time you sing it. (Examples: yellow chickies that peep, fluffy bunnies that hop)

Who did, who did, who did, who did,

Who did create swimming duckies?

Who did, who did, who did, who did,

Who did create swimming duckies?

God did, God did, God did, God did,

God created swimming duckies.

God created duckies,

God created duckies,

God created duckies—Quack!

by Lois Putnam

Four Seasons of a Garden

The children will learn all about planting and growing as they sing the words below to the tune of "Here We Go 'Round the Mulberry Bush" and act it out. (For more season fun, give the children a copy of page 14 to complete.)

(Walk slowly and pretend to take seeds out of one hand, dropping them as you sing.)

> This is the way we plant the seeds, plant the seeds, plant the seeds.
>
> This is the way we plant the seeds in the springtime season.

(Pretend you're hoeing while singing.)

> This is the way we hoe the plants, hoe the plants, hoe the plants.
>
> This is the way we hoe the plants in the summer season.

(Walk slowly, bending over to pretend to pick something, putting it in the "bowl" of your other arm.)

> This is the way we pick the food, pick the food, pick the food.
>
> This is the way we pick the food in the autumn season.

(Pretend to shovel snow while singing.)

> This is the way we shovel snow, shovel snow, shovel snow.
>
> This is the way we shovel snow in the winter season.

by Marcia Noel Hornok

In the Square

Toddlers will identify body parts as they play this game and sing this song.

Mark a square on the floor with masking tape. If you're outside, use a rope laid out to form a square.

Sing the following words to the tune of "London Bridge Is Falling Down." As they sing, toddlers should place the appropriate body part inside the square.

> Put your two hands in the square,
>
> In the square, in the square.
>
> Put your two hands in the square.
>
> Take them out now.
>
> Repeat, using "one foot," "two knees," "elbows," etc.
>
> For fun, let the children sing, "Put your teacher in the square."

Optional: Other shapes can be used, such as circle, triangle, rectangle, oval.

by Marcia Noel Hornok

Love That Never Ends

Sing the words below with the children to the tune of "The Song That Never Ends."

> This is the love that never ends.
> It just goes on and on, my friend.
> The Father started loving us before we were born,
> And now He keeps on loving us by sending us His Son.
>
> This is the love that never ends.
> It just goes on and on, my friend.
> The Father started loving us before we were born,
> And now He keeps on loving us by sending us His Son.

Sing the song over and over as many times as you like.

by Teresa Von Busch

A Counting Rhyme

One, one, let's have fun.

(Hold up one finger; stand up.)

Two, two, God made you.

(Hold up two fingers; point to others.)

Three, three, God made me.

(Hold up three fingers; point to self.)

Four, four, God made more.

(Hold up four fingers; point around.)

Five, five, we're alive.

(Hold up five fingers; move side to side.)

Six, six, a smile we'll fix.

(Hold up six fingers; trace a smile.)

Seven, seven, look up to heaven.

(Hold up seven fingers; look up.)

Eight, eight, God is great!

(Hold up eight fingers; spread arms wide.)

Nine, nine, get in line.

(Hold up nine fingers; make a line.)

Ten, ten, it's the end.

(Hold up ten fingers.)

by Lois Putnam

Movement: Stand in a circle for verses one–eight. Make a line for verses nine–ten.

Happy That You're You

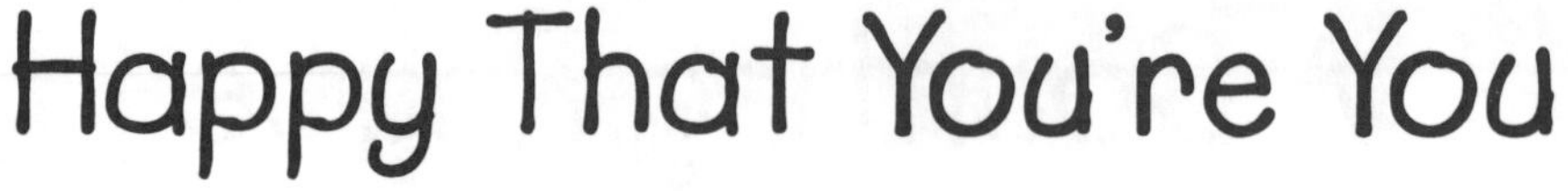

God made you;   (Point to a friend.)

God made me.   (Point to yourself.)

Now doesn't that make you   (Point to a friend.)

Happy as can be?   (Put on a big smiley face.)

When I love you,   (Point to yourself. Put hand on heart. Then point to a friend.)

And you love me,   (Point to a friend. Put hand on heart. Then point to yourself.)

That's the way   (Shake index finger.)

God meant it to be.   (Point toward heaven and nod head.)

by Susan Jordan